Original title:
The Owl's Frost

Copyright © 2024 Swan Charm
All rights reserved.

Author: Sara Säde
ISBN HARDBACK: 978-9908-52-950-9
ISBN PAPERBACK: 978-9908-52-951-6
ISBN EBOOK: 978-9908-52-952-3

## Hush of Ice-Kissed Pines

Whispers dance in frosty air,
Pines adorned with crystals fair.
Laughter echoes, spirits bright,
Underneath the moon's soft light.

Children play in snow's embrace,
Joyful smiles light up each face.
Warmth of hearts in chilly night,
Festive cheer, a pure delight.

## Celestial Watcher in the Wintry Realm

Stars above in velvet skies,
Glisten like a thousand eyes.
Snowflakes twirl, a graceful flight,
Nature's magic in the night.

Songs of joy, a crisp refrain,
Laughing winds through frosty grain.
Happiness wrapped, a cozy theme,
In the heart, a glowing dream.

## **Silhouette of Solitude**

In the quiet, shadows blend,
Solitary paths we wend.
Chilled but warm in thoughts we share,
Festive glow is everywhere.

Silhouettes against the glow,
Whispers carried through the snow.
Celebrate the peace we find,
In the stillness, hearts entwined.

## Frostbitten Dreams in Feathered Depths

Dreams arise like snowy flurries,
In soft whispers, no more worries.
Feathered depths, a gentle sway,
Frostbitten hopes light up the way.

Candles flicker, shadows play,
Mark the end of winter's day.
In the warmth of gathered kin,
Let the festive spirit in.

## Chill of the Midnight Vigil

Twinkling lights adorn the trees,
Laughter dances on the breeze.
Footprints trace the snowy ground,
Joyful echoes all around.

Candles flicker, shadows play,
Hearts unite on this bright day.
Stories shared by firelight,
Warmth outshines the winter's bite.

## **Celestial Wings in Frosted Air**

Stars above, a silver hue,
Frosted air whispers anew.
Children's laughter fills the night,
Dreams take off in pure delight.

Snowflakes dance in merry twirls,
Nature's magic gently swirls.
Each breath fogs in chilly air,
A festive breath, a moment rare.

## **Whispers of the Frigid Night**

Gentle hush of winter's breath,
Promises of joy beneath.
Gathered friends beneath the stars,
Celebration's light is ours.

Mirth in every single glance,
Cozy hearts in blissful trance.
Wrapped in warmth and love's embrace,
Festive smiles light up the space.

## **Tales from the Frostbitten Perch**

High above where the eagles soar,
Voices sing of yule and lore.
Ornaments dangle, a dazzling sight,
Sharing tales of warmth and light.

Hot cocoa steams in the cold,
Melodies of joy unfold.
As the night wraps us tight,
Hearts aglow in the starlight.

## A Midnight Watcher's Lament

In the stillness of night, bright stars align,
Whispers of joy drift through the pines.
Laughter echoes, sweet and clear,
Holding memories we all hold dear.

The moonlit path beckons us near,
With every heartbeat, we shed our fear.
Dancing shadows flicker and sway,
Winding through dreams of yesterday.

A toast to the night, our spirits soar,
In this moment, we are wanting more.
Shimmering glances, the world feels right,
We unite under this enchanting light.

## **Plumage in a Crystal World**

Snowflakes twirl like dancers spun,
Each a gem in the winter sun.
Colors burst in each joyous flurry,
Painting the earth in vibrant hurry.

With laughter we gather, hearts aglow,
In this kingdom where the soft winds blow.
Birds in bright plumage sing from above,
Echoing tales of winter love.

Frosted branches sparkle and gleam,
In this season, we weave our dream.
A chorus rises in sweet refrain,
As we celebrate through joy and pain.

## **Serene Shadows on Silver Snow**

Moonlight drapes a silver sheet,
Casting shadows where soft winds greet.
With gentle steps, we glide in tune,
Under the watchful eyes of the moon.

Stars flicker like candles in the sky,
Each a wish whispered, floating high.
Soft giggles dance on the chilly air,
Binding friends with love and care.

Breath of winter, crisp and bright,
Wraps us in warmth on this golden night.
A festive glow in every heart,
Reminding us, we'll never part.

## **Flight Beneath a Pale Harvest Moon**

Wings unfurl under moon's soft glow,
As fleeting moments begin to flow.
We chase the twilight, laughter high,
With the harvest moon framing our sky.

Firelight crackles, whispers rise,
Magic dances in starlit skies.
Each song carries dreams, deep and bold,
Stories of love and legends untold.

Through fields we wander, hand in hand,
Festive spirits illuminate the land.
Together we rise, the world in bloom,
Soaring free beneath the harvest moon.

## Keeper of the Winter's Secret

In the hush of white, the secrets lie,
Beneath the sparkle of the starlit sky.
Joyous laughter fills the frosty air,
As children play without a single care.

Twinkling lights adorn the evergreen,
Whispers of magic linger, softly seen.
Warmth of hearts in nights so cold,
Stories of wonder and dreams unfold.

Cocoa steaming in each little hand,
Fireside tales in a winter wonderland.
With each passing hour, spirits soar,
Together we gather, forevermore.

In the blanket of snow, we dance and sing,
Embracing the joy that the season brings.
Keeper of secrets, the winter does share,
A tapestry woven of love and care.

## Gaze of the Crystal Night

Stars shimmer bright in the velvet hue,
Moonlight dances on the frozen dew.
As laughter echoes through the crisp night,
Hearts ignite in the soft, warm light.

Candles flicker in the window's glow,
Inviting warmth from the world below.
The air is filled with a sweet delight,
Promises of joy in the crystal night.

Snowflakes twirl in a mesmerizing flight,
Whirling around under a sky so bright.
With each breath, magic fills the space,
In every smile, we see love's embrace.

Festive spirit wrapped in a gentle breeze,
Carrying laughter through the swaying trees.
In the hush of night, the world feels right,
Under the gaze of the crystal night.

## **Glacial Wings in the Stillness**

In the quiet hush of a winter's morn,
Where glacial wings of frost are born.
Every flake a story, every gleam a gift,
In the stillness, our spirits lift.

The air is crisp, the moments still,
With every breath, a gentle thrill.
Together we wander, hand in hand,
Creating memories in a snowy land.

Under the arch of a glimmering sky,
With laughter echoing, we soar high.
Each heartbeat basks in a shared delight,
Embraced by the magic of the night.

A festival of dreams, a wondrous sight,
In the glacial wings, we find our light.
Through the stillness, joy begins to gleam,
Together we weave our heartfelt dream.

**Night's Candor in Winter's Grasp**

In the embrace of winter's chilly kiss,
A time for joy, a moment of bliss.
With every flake that falls like a vow,
Night's candor speaks to the here and now.

Bonfires crackle as stories unfold,
Warmth surrounds, hearts never cold.
Together we gather, under starlit skies,
Gazing in wonder, with hopeful eyes.

The magic of night blankets the land,
In every heartbeat, the world feels grand.
As laughter dances on the frosty breeze,
In winter's grasp, we savor with ease.

Celebration flows in each smile and cheer,
Each moment cherished, with friends so dear.
Night's candor glows, a festive embrace,
A treasure of love in this wondrous place.

## **Wintry Eyes on Forgotten Trails**

On frosty paths where shadows play,
The snowflakes dance in bright array.
Laughter echoes through the trees,
As winter whispers on the breeze.

With every step, a memory blooms,
Underneath the chilly glooms.
In sparkling white, our spirits soar,
Awakening dreams from days of yore.

The twilight glows with twinkling lights,
Reflecting warmth in frigid nights.
With hearts alight, we forge ahead,
On wintry trails where joy is fed.

Together we chase the fading sun,
In frozen realms, our joys begun.
With every laugh and gentle cheer,
We weave a tapestry in the year.

## Mysterious Guardians of the Darkened Orchard

In moonlit groves where shadows sway,
The guardians keep the night at bay.
Whispers swirl like autumn leaves,
As magic weaves through boughs and eaves.

With silver glints on fruits so rare,
The orchard breathes its fragrant air.
Mysteries dance in each cool breeze,
In twilight's grip, our hearts appease.

Underneath the starry sky,
The guardians watch as dreams flit by.
In every rustle, secrets sigh,
As night unfolds its gentle tie.

With joy and laughter, we find our way,
Through shadows deep, where spirits play.
In this enchanted, hallowed space,
We share our hopes, our fears erase.

## Snow-Softened Secrets Cradle the Night

In blankets white, the world is still,
As soft snow falls on every hill.
Secrets whispered, low and clear,
Cradle the magic that draws us near.

Stars twinkle bright from heavens wide,
Illuminating paths we slide.
With joyful hearts, we take our flight,
Into the arms of winter's night.

Each flake a dream that we might hold,
In snow-blanketed stories told.
With laughter ringing through the air,
We share our warmth, a bond so rare.

As twilight deepens, shadows dance,
In moonlit gleams, we take our chance.
With snow-softened secrets in our care,
We find our joy beyond compare.

## Fluttering in the Frozen Lair

In the twilight glow, fairies dance,
Through icy groves, they take their chance.
Whispers of laughter in the crisp air,
Sparkling magic beyond compare.

Snowflakes twirl like confetti bright,
Each fluttering wing, a stunning sight.
Beneath the stars, in whimsy they play,
Such joy unleashed on this winter's day.

## Secrets of the Icy Canopy

Above, the branches wear cloaks of white,
Glistening jewels, a wondrous sight.
Hidden tales in the frost they hold,
Whispers of warmth in the bitter cold.

A serenade sung by the chilling breeze,
Swaying the boughs of the frosty trees.
Beneath this canopy, hearts entwine,
Finding solace in the crisp divine.

## Frost-Laden Branches and Muffled Calls

Branches heavy with blankets of snow,
Nature's whispers in tones soft and low.
The world, a canvas, painted in white,
As silence blankets the soft moonlight.

Muffled laughter from children at play,
Building their dreams in the snow today.
Each crunch of heel a joyous refrain,
Echoes of wonder in winter's domain.

## **Ethereal Silence Wraps the Woods**

In the stillness deep, magic unfurls,
Cascading snowflakes in gentle swirls.
Ethereal silence, a soothing balm,
Wrapping the woods in a peaceful calm.

Moonbeams dance on the surface of snow,
Guiding lost souls where dreams tend to grow.
In this serene embrace of the night,
Hearts find their rhythm, as spirits take flight.

## **Chilling Serenades of the Night**

Underneath the silver moon,
Laughter fills the frosty air.
Voices join in soft cocoon,
Melodies of joy to share.

Candles flicker, warmth ignites,
Snowflakes dance on whispered dreams.
In the hush, the heart invites,
Echoes of familiar themes.

Glistening stars like diamonds glow,
Friends gathering round the fire.
In the chill, spirits flow,
A symphony, we all conspire.

As the night begins to fade,
Wishes carried on the breeze.
With each song, new bonds are made,
Moments cherished, hearts at ease.

## Shadows Among the Icy Pines

Whispers weave through branches bare,
Carols echo, soft and sweet.
Flickering lights that paint the air,
As we gather, hearts repeat.

Footprints kiss the glistening ground,
Laughter mingles with the snow.
In this peace, our joy is found,
Time's embrace, a gentle flow.

Cups raised high, the toast begins,
Every story warm and bright.
In this moment, love just wins,
Magical is this winter night.

Shadows dance as embers glint,
Unified, we sing our song.
Grateful hearts, the air is pink,
In these shadows, we belong.

## **Echoes of the Winter Watcher**

Beneath the blanket, snow so deep,
Stars above like diamonds shine.
In this quiet, dreams we keep,
To the rhythm, hearts align.

Branches sway, the winds are light,
Chiming bells of festive cheer.
Gather round, embrace the night,
Moments cherished, ever near.

From the hearth, the warmth will spread,
Stories shared, our laughter flows.
Heavy hearts can find their lead,
In the glow, the spirit grows.

With the magic of the sky,
Fleeting time, yet love remains.
In the quiet, watch us fly,
Echoes dance in winter's chains.

## **Glistening Eyes in the Stillness**

In the stillness, lights aglow,
Wonders spark in every glance.
Joyful hearts beneath the snow,
In this space, we take our chance.

Glistening eyes, a twinkling sight,
Tales unfold, both new and old.
Together we make memories bright,
In the comfort, hands we hold.

Snowflakes fall like gentle dreams,
Wrapping warmth in frosty air.
In this moment, hope redeems,
Laughter echoes, love we share.

As the evening drapes its shawl,
In this wonder, we abide.
With each whisper, we enthrall,
In the stillness, hearts collide.

## In the Hush of the Snow-Woven Woods

In the hush of woods, snow falls slow,
Branches draped in white, all aglow.
Laughter lingers, merry and light,
A festive spirit dances in the night.

Candles flicker, casting warm beams,
Whispers amongst trees, like sweet dreams.
Footfalls crunch on the sparkling ground,
In this magic, joy's glow is found.

Families gather, hearts intertwined,
Happiness wrapped, in warmth confined.
A feast awaits beneath the stars,
Wishes are tossed like shooting czars.

In the silence, a whispering cheer,
Nature sings of joy, ever near.
In snow-woven woods, magic is spun,
Rejoicing together, hearts become one.

## Song of the Ice-Crafted Hunter

In the chill where the wild winds blow,
A hunter moves, with whispers low.
Ice-crafted dreams glimmer and shine,
Each step a beat in a festive line.

Under the veil of the shimmering night,
Stars twinkle down, the world feels right.
With laughter around the crackling fire,
The song of the ice lifts ever higher.

In the company of mates, tales unfold,
Warmth in their hearts, a spirit bold.
Through valleys and peaks, the echoes call,
Each story shared, a festival for all.

As twilight fades and shadows play,
The joy of the night then finds its way.
With every breath wrapped in delight,
The hunter moves, embracing the night.

## **Twilight Secrets in Feathered Faces**

In twilight's glow, secrets take flight,
Feathered faces shimmer, pure delight.
Stories weave through the dusk-lit trees,
Echoing laughter borne from the breeze.

Festive whispers on the wings of fate,
Birds sing sweetly, as if to celebrate.
In every flutter, joy is unfurled,
Bringing life to the hush of the world.

Adorned in colors that sparkle and gleam,
Nature unfolds in a merry dream.
Under the stars, the magic begins,
With each gentle note, a new song spins.

Wings brush softly, like kisses on skin,
Inviting all listeners to join in.
In feathered faces, joy finds its place,
Twilight's secrets in a warm embrace.

## Echoing Twilight's Frosted Breath

In twilight's realm, the air feels true,
With frosted breath, dreams come into view.
Luminous glows twinkle from afar,
Echoing magic like a shimmering star.

Children dance with laughter unbound,
Chasing the tales that enchant the ground.
Joyful hearts beat in rhythm and cheer,
As festive spirits draw loved ones near.

The night weaves spells, glowing and bright,
Each corner whispers, adorned in light.
Snowflakes twirl in a jubilant play,
As echoes of laughter fade not away.

In the twilight, friendships interlace,
Holding close love's warm embrace.
With frosted breath, let all spirits rise,
In the echo of joy, where happiness lies.

# **Frosted Reverence in Long Shadows**

Glimmers dance on winter's breath,
As laughter curls in frosty air.
Children play where shadows rest,
In a world that's bright and rare.

Twinkling lights adorn the trees,
Whispers light the dusky skies.
Joyful hearts ride on the breeze,
As warmth ignites in every sigh.

Candles flicker, spirits roar,
Mirthful songs rise with the night.
Every soul will come to adore,
This season wrapped in pure delight.

Frosted dreams in moonlit grace,
Hand in hand, we weave our tales.
In this enchanted, magical place,
Where love and laughter fill the pales.

# The Whispering Glade

In the glade where secrets play,
Nature hums a merry tune.
Leaves of gold and skies of gray,
Underneath the silver moon.

Bubbles rise from winter streams,
Echoing the joy we share.
Each soft sigh a whisper beams,
Wrapped in warmth, beyond compare.

Footsteps crunch on frosted ground,
While fireflies light the way.
Laughter mingles all around,
As we gather, night must sway.

From the shadows, dreams emerge,
Sparkling like the stars above.
In this moment, hearts converge,
In the glade, we toast to love.

## Vigilant Heart of Night's Realm

The moon stands guard, a watchful eye,
As stars twinkle in velvet skies.
Night breathes deep, a quiet sigh,
While joy and peace softly rise.

Echoes of laughter fill the air,
With warmth that breaks the winter chill.
Christmas lights burn bright and fair,
While soft hoots of owls instill.

Hearts entwined in fleeting dance,
Feel the pulse of stories told.
In this moment, lost in trance,
Under night's embrace so bold.

With every whisper, hopes ignite,
In the realm where dreams take flight.
The vigilant heart of the night,
Keeps our spirits warm and bright.

## **Across the Icy Expanse**

Across the ice, our spirits glide,
In a world of shimmering light.
Laughter echoes, joy our guide,
As stars twinkle, a beautiful sight.

Snowflakes twirl in playful dance,
Underneath the moon's soft glow.
Each moment takes us by chance,
In this wonderland, spirits grow.

With every step, we carve our dreams,
In the glistening, pristine ground.
Frosted laughter, soft moonbeams,
In this magic, we are found.

Together we embrace the chill,
Hearts aglow with festive cheer.
Across the expanse, all is still,
As we cherish all we hold dear.

# Whispers of Winter Wings

Snowflakes dance on breezes light,
A shimmered world, so pure and bright.
Children laugh with hearts so warm,
In winter's magic, they find charm.

Icicles hang like crystal glass,
Each breath of joy, the moments pass.
Trees adorned in white attire,
Underneath the stars' soft fire.

The cocoa warms our chilly hands,
As laughter rings in joyful bands.
With every twirl, in the fresh air,
We celebrate with love so rare.

As shadows play beneath the moon,
Our hearts unite in joyous tune.
Whispers of winter, sweet and clear,
In this bright season, love draws near.

## Midnight's Silent Embrace

Starlight twinkles, a diamond hue,
Wrapped in warmth, just me and you.
Underneath the velvet skies,
Our hopes and dreams begin to rise.

The night invites with a gentle breeze,
Rustling leaves and swaying trees.
A serenade of nature's song,
In midnight's hold, we both belong.

With lanterns glowing, shadows play,
As laughter sparkles through the fray.
A warmth that hushes all despair,
In midnight's embrace, love fills the air.

Around the fire, we share our tales,
As starlit wishes set our sails.
In this moment, so divine,
Midnight's magic, yours and mine.

**Frosted Feathers in Moonlight**

Softly glistening, the world transformed,
While silver beams of moonlight warmed.
Frosted feathers, a gentle sight,
In nature's hush, all feels right.

Whispers of owls in the trees,
Echo softly on the breeze.
Snowy paths and laughter blend,
In winter's charm, all worries mend.

With every flake, a new delight,
Painting dreams in the still of night.
Through frosted whispers, love will soar,
Every heartbeat, we adore.

Moments wrapped in starlit glow,
As crystal snowflakes gently flow.
Frosted feathers, soft and light,
Guide us through this wondrous night.

## **Hoots Beneath a Crystal Sky**

The night unveils its jeweled crown,
While hoots of owls twirl all around.
Beneath a sky of endless dreams,
The world awakens in starry beams.

Snowy hills invite a glide,
With frosty laughter, hearts open wide.
Each moment, a magical spree,
As joy paints smiles, wild and free.

Around the fire, stories flow,
The warmth of friendship starts to glow.
With every cheer and festive sound,
In winter's heart, our love is found.

Through dancing lights, a gentle cheer,
In this season, all hold dear.
Hoots beneath a crystal sky,
Together we celebrate, you and I.

## An Icy Ballet under the Full Moon

Under the moon's bright, silver glow,
Snowflakes twirl, a graceful show.
The world is hushed, a night so still,
Caught in beauty, hearts do thrill.

Dancers glide on the frozen floor,
Whispers of magic, forevermore.
The stars above join the twinkling spree,
As winter's rhythm sets spirits free.

## **The Forest's Chilling Embrace**

In the woods where shadows play,
Snow-draped branches sway and sway.
Echoes of laughter ride the breeze,
Nature wrapped in silken freeze.

Lights flicker through the frosty pines,
Joy dances in the starlit lines.
Voices blend with the nightingale,
Weaving stories, a festive tale.

## Muffled Mysteries of the Twilight Hour

As daylight fades, the twilight glows,
Glimmers of joy in the winter snows.
A candle's flicker, a warm embrace,
Muffled laughter fills the space.

The secrets hide in a snowy hush,
Moments cherished, sweet and plush.
In every shadow, stories unfold,
Of hopes and dreams, both new and old.

## **Serenade of Frigid Feathers**

Feathers fall, a soft cascade,
Adorn the ground in a snow-white parade.
Whispers find their path on high,
A serenade beneath the sky.

Jubilant hearts in coats of warmth,
Spin and twirl, a winter's charm.
As firelight dances in each gaze,
Together we celebrate these days.

## **Perched on a Bitter Branch**

Colors dance in twilight's glow,
Laughter echoes, spirits flow.
Joyful hearts in vibrant throng,
Sing together, life is song.

Fireflies twinkle, stars ignite,
Underneath the moon's soft light.
Bitter branches hold their sway,
While we cheer the night away.

Candles flicker, wishes soar,
Every moment begs for more.
With each chime, the world feels right,
Hopeful whispers fill the night.

Together we find love and peace,
In this fest of sweet release.
Perched high on joy's embrace,
Life's celebrations quicken pace.

# **Glacial Whispers in the Dark**

Through the snow, the laughter beams,
Glacial whispers weave our dreams.
Frosty air, yet hearts feel warm,
Together we withstand the storm.

Winter's breath, a festive tune,
Moonlight dances, bright as noon.
In the quiet, we take flight,
On this magical, wintry night.

Branches glisten, crystals sway,
Every moment feels like play.
Hand in hand, we weave the night,
Sharing stories, pure delight.

Frozen pathways, tales unfold,
In our laughter, warmth is gold.
With each word, the darkness fades,
In the echoes, friendship wades.

## **Eternal Stillness in Feathered Eyes**

In the stillness, wings take flight,
Feathered friends in soft moonlight.
Nature sings a gentle tune,
Festive tones of blissful June.

Whispers carried on the breeze,
Joyful melodies through the trees.
Eyes that sparkle, bright and wise,
Eternal stillness in their eyes.

Gathered close, we find our cheer,
In the laughter, love draws near.
Hearts entwined in nature's call,
United, we shall never fall.

Through the night, the echoes ring,
Life's embrace, our hearts will sing.
In this moment, pure and bright,
We find magic in the night.

## The Chill of Wisdom Unfurled

Amidst the warmth, a chill resides,
Wisdom waits where love abides.
Festive tales from ages past,
In the shadows, spells are cast.

Gather 'round, the fire glows,
Voices rise as friendship grows.
Every story, wrapped in light,
Brings us joy, through the night.

Through the chill, we learn to thrive,
In laughter's embrace, we come alive.
Echoes of the wise remain,
Chasing sorrow, easing pain.

With every cheer, together we stand,
Hand in hand, across the land.
In this moment, life reveals,
Joyful hearts and love that heals.

## **Enigmatic Eyes in the Chill**

In the evening's soft embrace,
Twinkling lights begin to glow.
Laughter dances in the air,
As the winter winds blow slow.

Children gather, spirits bright,
Snowflakes twirl like joyful streams.
Whispers shared by firelight,
Warming hearts and glowing dreams.

Underneath the moonlit skies,
Enigmatic eyes hold sway.
Glistening like stars on high,
Guiding all who come to play.

Joyous songs take flight and soar,
Melodies of love and cheer.
With each note, we seek for more,
In this festive time of year.

## **Silver Cloak of the Night Hunter**

Beneath the silver cloak of night,
Whispers call the skies above.
The hunter moves with quiet grace,
As the world spins with pure love.

Stars like jewels in velvet wear,
Guide the footsteps in the dark.
In this realm where dreams unfold,
Echoes of laughter leave a mark.

Fires crackle, shadows play,
Around a circle, friends unite.
In this magic, spirits sway,
Illuminated by the light.

With every tale, the evening grows,
A tapestry of life and cheer.
Underneath the moon's soft glow,
The night hunter draws us near.

## **Frosted Pines and Silent Shadows**

Amongst the frosted pines we roam,
Where silence drapes like a shawl.
Each breath crystallizes in the air,
As winter's beauty casts a thrall.

Shadows dance in silver light,
Creating wonders, pure delight.
Nature's canvas, vast and bright,
Holds festivity through the night.

With snowflakes swirling, children play,
Building dreams of white and glee.
In the hush, they laugh and sway,
Carving joy for all to see.

The world adorned in sparkling white,
Whispers secrets of the trees.
Frosted pines and silent night,
Bring us together in the freeze.

## **The Guardian of Frosted Woods**

Deep in the forest, soft and wide,
A guardian stands, gentle and wise.
With frosted breath and watchful eyes,
He keeps the cheer and love inside.

Around the trees, the whispers sing,
Of friendships forged in winter's embrace.
With every step, the joy we bring,
Is woven tight in this sacred place.

Candles flicker in the night,
Casting warmth on each cold stone.
In this space, everything feels right,
In the heart's sanctuary, we're not alone.

So gather close, let spirits rise,
With laughter, warmth, and quiet glee.
The guardian smiles as snowflakes fly,
In the frosted woods, we are free.

## **Secrets Told in Snowy Silence**

Snowflakes descend with a shimmer bright,
Whispers of joy on a starry night.
Laughter echoes through the frosty air,
Dreams take flight, free from every care.

Children gather with a twinkling glee,
Building castles, a sight to see.
Every flake tells a story sweet,
In this winter wonder, hearts skip a beat.

Crackling fire in a lantern's glow,
Voices mingle as the breezes blow.
Underneath blankets, warmth they find,
Together they leave their cares behind.

Carols ring out, a melodic cheer,
Filling the night with festivities near.
Secrets whispered in the soft night air,
In the snowy silence, love's everywhere.

## **The Veil of Winter's Watcher**

A blanket of white hides the earth's embrace,
Winter's watcher smiles with a gentle grace.
Stars twinkle brightly, a dazzling show,
While shadows dance softly in the moon's glow.

Twinkling lights adorn every tree,
Gifts of the season, so joyful and free.
Warmth in our hearts as we share and connect,
In the silence of snow, we feel its effect.

Fireside chats with cocoa so sweet,
Gathered together, a seasonal treat.
Laughter and stories flow like the stream,
Under the watcher's soft, luminous beam.

With every snowflake, a wish takes flight,
Uniting our spirits this magical night.
The veil of winter wraps us all tight,
In the glow of the stars, everything feels right.

# **Whispers of Winter Wings**

Gentle whispers of the winter's air,
Carry secrets no one can compare.
Feathers of frost dance on every tree,
Charming the world with their mystery.

Snow-laden branches form a crystal line,
In this winter's Eden, all feels divine.
Every soft flake, a delicate tune,
Playing the symphony of the silver moon.

Footprints crisscross in patterns unique,
A festive journey, the joy we seek.
With every movement, laughter ignites,
As we race through the magic of winter nights.

In the stillness, nature's breath sings,
Enveloping us with the warmth it brings.
As winter's wings flutter and roam,
We find in this season, a true sense of home.

## Moonlit Vigil in the Forest

Under the moon's soft, silvery glow,
The forest awakens with whispers low.
Every tree wears a cloak of white lace,
Nature's beauty, a serene embrace.

Footsteps crunch on the blanket of snow,
Magic surrounds us, a mystical flow.
In the stillness, the world holds its breath,
As we gather warmth in this night of depth.

Stars sprinkle down from the heavens above,
Illuminating the moments we love.
Around the fire, our stories are spun,
In the moonlit vigil, we feel as one.

The chill of the night is combated by cheer,
With every laugh, the warmth draws near.
In this winter's night, our hearts intertwine,
Under the moon's watch, everything's fine.

**Eyes Like Lanterns**

In the crowd, they sparkle bright,
Dancing flames in the soft twilight.
Laughter rings, a joyous sound,
Where every heart finds joy unbound.

Shadows play beneath bright lights,
Magic woven, sweet delights.
Hands held close, the warmth we share,
In each moment, love laid bare.

Colors swirl in the cheerful air,
Every glance a whispered prayer.
Joyous spirits rise and sing,
In this wonder, our hearts cling.

Underneath a canvas sky,
We let our dreams and hopes fly high.
Together as the evening glows,
In the warmth, our spirits flow.

## **Chilled Echoes of the Night**

Stars twinkle in the chilly air,
Whispers float, a loving care.
Footsteps dance on frosty ground,
In the dark, our joy is found.

Echoes vibrant, laughter shared,
In every heartbeat, we have dared.
Candlelight flickers, soft and bright,
Guiding us through this festive night.

Moonbeams paint a silver hue,
While memories weave bright and true.
In this moment, we are free,
Together 'neath the elder trees.

Chilled but warm, we gather close,
In every toast, we raise, we boast.
For every echo sings our name,
Unified in love's sweet flame.

## **Feathers Against the Silent Sky**

A carnival, bright and bold,
With stories waiting to be told.
Feathers float upon the breeze,
Gentle whispers, hearts at ease.

In the twilight, tales ignite,
Laughter dances, pure delight.
Each moment cherished, never shy,
As dreams take flight in the night sky.

Faces bright with painted grace,
Joyful steps, a bustling space.
Underneath the stars so high,
We celebrate, let spirits fly.

Every cheer and shared embrace,
In this weave, we find our place.
With feathers soft against the glow,
In festive warmth, our love will grow.

## **Frosted Secrets at Twilight**

Whispers linger in the cold,
Frosted secrets yet untold.
Twilight's hue, a soft embrace,
As hopes unfold in this sacred space.

Stars emerge, the night awakes,
Every joy that laughter makes.
Underneath the crystal glow,
Together, hearts begin to flow.

In this moment, time stands still,
With every heartbeat, we fulfill.
Windows frosted, smiles so wide,
We gather here with love and pride.

Fires crackle, embers bright,
Sharing dreams on this lovely night.
In fleeting time, let stories rise,
Frosted secrets, in joy, surprise.

# **Icy Lullabies of the Night**

Whispers dance on frosty air,
Snowflakes twirl without a care.
Stars above begin to gleam,
Underneath the silver dream.

Children's laughter fills the skies,
Joy reflected in their eyes.
Cocoa warms in cozy nooks,
As firelight plays in storybooks.

The moon casts down a gentle light,
Guiding hearts on this festive night.
Softly wrapped in winter's song,
In this magic, we belong.

Every flake a wish sent high,
In this moment, time will fly.
Let the snowflakes gently fall,
Icy lullabies, wrapping all.

## **Shadows of the Veiled One**

Mysteries whisper in the night,
Shadows dance in soft moonlight.
Figures sway beneath the trees,
Wrapped in secrets, carried breeze.

Lanterns glow with amber hue,
Illuminating paths so true.
Veiled one smiles behind her mask,
In the festive night, we bask.

Echoes of laughter fill the air,
Sharing tales, moments rare.
Hands are clasped in joy and mirth,
Together, we celebrate our worth.

Through the veils, a warmth ignites,
Bringing clarity to the nights.
In each shadow, love resides,
Festivities where truth abides.

# Murmurs Beneath the Ice-laden Branches

A hush falls deep within the woods,
Where joyous hearts forget their broods.
Ice-laden branches softly creak,
Whispers of winter, calm yet sleek.

Footsteps crunch on frosty ground,
Magic in the air is found.
Skaters glide on glimmering ice,
With laughter sweet, their hearts entice.

Lights are strung on every tree,
Twinkling bright, a jubilee.
Underneath the icy bows,
Peaceful moments, joy bestows.

Murmurs rise as spirits cheer,
Embracing warmth this time of year.
Beneath each branch, together we sing,
Celebrating all that love can bring.

## Frost-kissed Echoes in the Twilight

Twilight settles, a breath serene,
Frost-kissed echoes, winter's sheen.
Candles flicker in the night,
As hopes take flight in pure delight.

Softly sung, carols rise,
Melodies weave 'neath starlit skies.
Families gather, warm and near,
In the magic of this year.

Snowflakes dance in swirling grace,
Each one unique in its embrace.
Laughter bursts like joyous song,
In the glow where we belong.

With every heartbeat, spirits soar,
Together, we are evermore.
Frost-kissed echoes whisper bold,
Tales of joy and love retold.

## Sentry of the Night's Embrace

Dancing lights twinkle bright,
Laughter fills the chilled air,
Joy wraps round like a cloak,
Stars join the festive affair.

Cider warms the winter hearts,
Children's glee, a lively song,
Snowflakes whirl in playful gusts,
Together we all belong.

The moon casts shadows, soft and light,
Carols echo through the pines,
Each moment sparkles like the frost,
Harmony in joyous lines.

With whispers of the night's embrace,
We gather close, our spirits soar,
In unity, we find our grace,
Tonight, forever, we explore.

## **Frostbitten Murmurs Among Ancient Trees**

Beneath the branches, whispers rise,
Frost-kissed leaves twinkle bright,
Gathered round, we share our dreams,
Hope shines through the wintry night.

Beneath the stars, the stories flow,
Each laugh, a promise, bright and clear,
The scent of pine and cinnamon,
Wraps us like a warm, sweet cheer.

Moonlit shadows dance and sway,
Echoing the heart's delight,
Together we weave memories,
In the glow of the firelight.

Nature sings her frosty tune,
United in the chill, we gleam,
Embracing all that winter brings,
We celebrate a shared dream.

## In the Embrace of Winter's Guardian

The winter guardian stands so tall,
Wrapping us in frosty peace,
With every flake, the world feels new,
In winter's embrace, all woes cease.

Crisp air dances with our cheer,
Firelight flickers, shadows play,
In every smile, warmth is found,
Together we banish the gray.

Mirth and stories fill the night,
Chilled fingers clutch warm cups tight,
An ancient bond, we celebrate,
As joy ignites the dark with light.

In laughter, echoes of the past,
We toast to the time we share,
Under the watch of endless stars,
Wrapped in love, we breathe the air.

# Timeless Watcher beneath the Frozen Sky

Beneath the vast and frozen sky,
A timeless watcher, bright and bold,
Guides us through the winter's night,
With tales of joy and warmth retold.

The candles flicker in the breeze,
While snowflakes dance on hidden paths,
Each sparkle mirrors our delight,
In this moment, laughter lasts.

Season of chill and warmth combined,
Where friendships blossom in the frost,
Together, we build memories,
In the embrace of what is lost.

Here beneath this frozen dome,
Our spirits soar, as hearts align,
In the magic of the night's embrace,
We find our peace, our souls entwined.

## **Frozen Feathers**

Snowflakes dance on a gentle breeze,
Whispers of joy among the trees.
Laughter emerges, bright and clear,
As winter's magic draws us near.

Warm cocoa in our eager hands,
Hearts unite in snowy lands.
With every twirl, each child spins,
Creating tales where wonder begins.

Glistening trails of shimmering white,
Under the stars, the world feels right.
From frosty breath to glowing smiles,
We cherish moments that fill the miles.

In the cozy glow, we gather tight,
Tales of adventure, the sheer delight.
This festive air, like a soft embrace,
Fills our souls, gives life a grace.

## **Silent Songs**

As night falls, the silence sings,
Nature wrapped in peace it brings.
Moonlight drapes the earth so soft,
While starlit dreams drift high aloft.

Footprints whisper on the snow,
Stories hidden, lost to flow.
Voices of joy in the crisp, cool air,
Echoes found everywhere we dare.

Candles flicker, shadows sway,
Our hearts rejoice in this display.
With every smile, a bond is spun,
In festive nights, we are as one.

Let laughter reign, let spirits soar,
With open hearts, we find much more.
Silent songs of the world unite,
In winter's wonder, all feels right.

## The Chill of Night's Caress

Beneath the stars, the chill sets in,
A tender touch, a whispered din.
Frosty air fills every space,
With winter's charm, we find our place.

Laughter bubbles, it lightly flows,
As breath turns white in dazzling shows.
Friends come together, sharing cheer,
Pouring warmth in each icy sphere.

The night embraces, soft and kind,
In every glance, true joy we find.
With every giggle and dance of grace,
The chill lifts hearts, a warm embrace.

Celebration shines, bright and bold,
Stories of memories waiting to be told.
In the caress of night so deep,
We weave together dreams we keep.

## **Reflections in Ice-Covered Eyes**

Glittering flakes fall through the sky,
Children gaze up, wonder drawn nigh.
Their eyes sparkle, catching light,
In the chill of this magical night.

Mirrors of joy, they brightly gleam,
Each frosty breath, a hopeful dream.
Laughter echoes in the shimmering glow,
As winter weaves its soothing flow.

Fires crackle, warmth reaches wide,
In shared delight, we take our stride.
With stories spinning in the holiday air,
We celebrate together, nothing can compare.

In the depth of winter's silver hue,
Reflections of love, steadfast and true.
In every heart, a sparkling sigh,
In ice-covered eyes, our spirits fly.

## **Beneath the Mirth of Winter's Shroud**

Winter's shroud wraps the world so tight,
Drifting snowflakes blanket the night.
Happiness glows in twinkling lights,
As we gather 'round to share delights.

The soft crunch of boots on snow,
Excitement bubbles, emotions flow.
In every hug, warmth to disperse,
Among friends united, we converse.

Cider warms us, sweet and bold,
In every sip, stories unfold.
With laughter ringing in frosty air,
The spirit of joy is everywhere.

Beneath this shroud, we make our way,
In festive spirit, we laugh and play.
Through winter nights, together we roam,
Finding in each heart, a place called home.

## **Nightfall's Feathered Guardian**

In twilight's glow, the feathers gleam,
A guardian soars above the stream.
With wings spread wide, it graces night,
A dance of shadows, pure delight.

The stars alight, they twinkle bright,
In harmony with the soothing night.
Chirps and whispers fill the air,
Joy and laughter everywhere.

Beneath the trees, so tall and grand,
Festivities born from nature's hand.
The gentle breeze joins in the fun,
As day departs, and night's begun.

So raise your glass to skies that glow,
To nightfall's charm and the moonlight's show.
With feathered friends, we celebrate,
Under the stars, we dance and wait.

## A Dance of Frost and Silence

Crisp are the nights, a frosty plea,
In the quiet corners, joy runs free.
Snowflakes swirl in silver bliss,
Each flake a secret, a frosty kiss.

The world adorned in white attire,
With glimmering lights that inspire.
In whispered tones, we twirl and sway,
Under the stars, we dance away.

A gentle hush blankets the ground,
With each step taken, joy is found.
Together we laugh, our spirits soar,
In this frozen night, we crave for more.

So come, let's weave a tale so bright,
In the dance of frost, our hearts take flight.
As silence sings its sweet refrain,
We celebrate love in winter's reign.

## **The Frosted Watcher's Call**

Upon the hill, a watcher stands,
With frosted breath, it grips the lands.
In quiet moments, it calls our name,
To join the dance, to feel the flame.

Beneath the moon, so soft and round,
Whispers of joy weave through the ground.
Each note a promise, a festive cheer,
With every heartbeat, the light draws near.

A tapestry of dreams unfolds,
In silver threads, our story told.
The watcher smiles, its gaze sincere,
Inviting all to gather here.

In the frosted air, our laughter rings,
As we embrace what this moment brings.
A symphony of hearts entwined,
The frosted watcher, forever kind.

## Secrets in the Glaze of Moonlight

Beneath the moon, the world aglow,
Secrets whispered in ebb and flow.
In soft caress of night's embrace,
We dance and twirl in timeless grace.

With every glance, a spark ignites,
In silken shadows, hearts take flight.
The glaze of gold on leaves so bright,
Invites our souls to join the night.

A jubilant chorus fills the air,
As laughter echoes everywhere.
The magic swirls, a festive song,
In moonlight's grasp, where we belong.

So gather close, let joy unfold,
In secrets shared, the night's retold.
With every heartbeat, we become,
A tapestry of love, in moonlight spun.

## **Guardians of the Frozen Shadows**

In the icy realm where whispers play,
The guardians dance in a shimmering sway.
Laughter echoes through the frosty glade,
As twinkling stars in night's embrace fade.

With every step, the snowflakes gleam,
In festive joy, they swirl and beam.
The moonlight bathes their frosted skin,
Inviting all who believe within.

Around the fire, stories unfold,
Of ancient legends and hearts of gold.
The chill of winter, a warming delight,
These frozen shadows, alive with light.

So raise a glass to the winter cheer,
To the guardians that bring us near.
In every heartbeat, the magic flows,
In the frozen shadows, anything glows.

## **Nightfall's Ebon Emissary**

As twilight dances on the velvet sky,
The emissary calls with a gentle sigh.
With each flicker, the lanterns ignite,
Warming the souls on this crisp night.

Beneath the stars, the singed sparks rise,
Echoing laughter from hills to the skies.
The crisp air hums with a festive tune,
Painting the night with the glow of the moon.

Joyful whispers weave through the trees,
As revelers sway on a wintry breeze.
A tapestry woven from joy and delight,
Celebrating the magic of night's endless flight.

So hold your loved ones beneath the stars,
Embrace the warmth that comes from afar.
For in this night, we all belong,
As nightfall sings its vibrant song.

## **Beneath the Glaze of Winter's Breath**

Beneath the glaze that winter weaves,
Nature sparkles, while joy believes.
Each flurry twirls with laughter bright,
A carnival of shimmering light.

Frosty branches, twinkling fair,
Invite the world to pause and stare.
With every breath, a cloud of bliss,
In this moment, we find our kiss.

Children's voices fill the air,
Building dreams with snow to share.
A joyous chorus in crystal white,
United under the winter's plight.

So dance beneath this frosty sky,
Let your spirit soar, let worries fly.
For in this season of joyful mirth,
We celebrate the beauty of our Earth.

## **Veil of Frost Over Ancient Eyes**

A veil of frost cloaks the olden trees,
Whispered tales carried by the breeze.
Ancient eyes twinkle with memories bright,
A festooned celebration this winter night.

The moon drapes silver over frozen ground,
As magic stirs in silence profound.
In every glance, a spark of delight,
Woven shadows dance in the pale moonlight.

Candles flicker, casting warmth anew,
In this serene night where dreams come true.
The earth dons its cloak of shimmering white,
As hearts unite in the soft glow of twilight.

So gather round, let the stories unfold,
In the embrace of winter's purest gold.
For beneath this veil, all things align,
In the heart of the night, let love brightly shine.

## Embrace of the Winter Sentinel

In the hush of a snowy night,
Stars flicker, dazzling and bright.
The air sparkles, a magical breath,
Embracing the warmth in winter's sheath.

Children's laughter, echoes of cheer,
Joyful hearts, spreading near.
Snowflakes dance, a twinkling ballet,
As dreams unfold in a festive array.

Candles glow, casting soft light,
Whispers of love, a cozy delight.
Around the fire, stories ignite,
In the embrace of winter's night.

Join the celebration, let spirits soar,
Together we cherish, forever more.
In this season, let happiness take flight,
Under the watch of the winter sentinel's light.

## Secrets Linger in Crystal Light

Through the trees, a pathway glows,
As twilight weaves its crystal shows.
Secrets hidden in frosty twirl,
Enchanting whispers begin to unfurl.

Glistening branches, adorned with dreams,
Reflect the joy in moonlit beams.
With every breath, a promise sings,
In the magic that this season brings.

Snowflakes fall like gentle sighs,
Into the night, where wonder lies.
Underneath the starry skies,
We find the truth in joyful eyes.

So gather close, let warmth ignite,
In the glow of this crystal light.
For within these moments, hearts align,
As secrets linger, pure and divine.

## **Glimpse of Wisdom on Frosty Wings**

A soft breath whispers through the pines,
Echoes of wisdom in icy designs.
Frosty wings take flight with grace,
Carrying tales through a quiet space.

Among the shadows, wisdom dances,
In the heart of winter, love enhances.
Each flake that falls, a lesson true,
Reminding us of magic anew.

Winds weave stories, old and wise,
Sparking joy beneath the frosty skies.
With every turn, hope takes its stand,
In the whispers of winter's hand.

So let us bask in this serene glow,
Learning from nature's ebb and flow.
For in the silence, our hearts will sing,
Of the wisdom found on frosty wings.

## Serpent of the Night in a White Realm

In the twilight of winter's grace,
A serpent slithers, leaving no trace.
Through the landscape, white and bright,
It weaves a spell in the chilly night.

Its scales shimmer like stars in the dark,
Each movement a song, a festive spark.
In this realm of frost, we dance along,
To the whispers of nature's song.

Around the bonfire, spirits unite,
Embracing the magic of the night.
The serpent coils with joyful cheer,
Binding us close, drawing us near.

With the shimmer of snow, dreams take flight,
In the enchanting world of the winter's night.
Join the festivity, let laughter swell,
In the embrace of this white, wondrous spell.

## **Nocturnal Tales Beneath Icebound Stars**

Under a quilt of shimmering night,
Whispers of joy take playful flight.
Frosty laughter in the cool breeze,
Dancing lights sway among the trees.

Beneath the moon's gentle embrace,
Dreamers gather in this sacred space.
With every twinkle, a story unfolds,
Of hidden treasures and tales retold.

Glistening icicles hang like gems,
Frozen echoes of woodland hymns.
Hope and wonder intertwine,
As the stars in their glory align.

From shadows arise, the frosty friends,
Unveiling the magic that never ends.
In this nocturnal realm so divine,
Every heart sings in pure design.

## **A Bough of Crystalized Silence**

On branches heavy with glistening dew,
A bough adorned, a wondrous view.
Soft whispers blend with the moonlight's glow,
In silence, a celebration begins to flow.

Snowflakes twirl in a jubilant dance,
Each flake a spark of fleeting chance.
Laughter drifts through the crisp, cold air,
Joy and magic are everywhere.

A veil of frost blankets the land,
Holding the warmth of a friendly hand.
Harmonies rise from the winter's hold,
Tales of the heart in letters of gold.

Embroidered lights on each window frame,
Echoing softly of love's sweet name.
In the stillness, the world feels right,
Wrapped in the charm of this frozen night.

## **Glistening Gaze of the Enigmatic**

Amidst the glimmer, shadows arise,
Glimmering wonders before our eyes.
In every corner, a secret waits,
Wrapped in the light of shimmering fates.

Curious hearts wander, bodies entwined,
In the embrace of the night, unconfined.
Flashes of laughter illuminate the dark,
As kindred spirits ignite their spark.

The whispers of stars, they beckon near,
Filling the air with warmth and cheer.
As midnight's song takes flight on the breeze,
Swaying softly, like swaying trees.

In this twilight realm where dreams collide,
There's magic alive that we cannot hide.
With every breath, the mystery sings,
Of glistening gazes and wondrous things.

## **Lullabies of the Frostbound Night**

In frosty stillness, the lullabies hum,
Echoes of love as hearts become one.
Veils of white over fields so wide,
Cradled in warmth, we take our stride.

Crystalline whispers brush against skin,
Awakening spirits, where dreams begin.
Each note of the night a gentle embrace,
Guiding us forth to a magical place.

Fireside tales wrapped in knitted seams,
Flickering light dances with dreams.
Through windows aglow, the world feels bright,
As we settle in for the frostbound night.

Memories woven in threads of delight,
In this festive haven, everything's right.
With lullabies sung beneath the sky,
The magic of winter will never die.

# Enigma in Every Flake

Drifting softly from the sky,
A dance of white, oh how they fly.
Each flake bears secrets, sublime and bright,
Whispers of magic in the moonlight.

Children laugh, they catch the snow,
In their hands, pure joy will grow.
A symphony of shimmering light,
Enigmas twirl in the chilly night.

The world adorned in a festive hue,
Nature's canvas, forever anew.
In the stillness, the moment stays,
A wonderland, where hearts can play.

Embrace the chill with open arms,
In every flake, a world of charms.
Together we dance, beneath the trees,
With frosted dreams carried on the breeze.

**Frosted Dreams on Frosted Wings**

Underneath a starry dome,
Wings of frost carry dreams back home.
Whispers of joy in the frosty air,
Magic lingers everywhere.

Snowflakes twirl on playful winds,
In laughter and cheer, a story begins.
Each breath is visible, a tender kiss,
In the stillness, we find our bliss.

Beneath the blanket of glistening white,
The world glows softly, hearts feel light.
In this holiday, we find our song,
With frosted dreams where we all belong.

Wings of wonder lift us high,
Together we soar, just you and I.
As starlight kisses the snow-kissed ground,
In every heartbeat, joy can be found.

## The Stillness Knew My Name

In the silence of winter's embrace,
The stillness knew my name, a gentle grace.
Snowflakes gathered, a whispering choir,
Bathing the world in softest attire.

Footprints mark a journey so rare,
Wandering dreams that swirl in the air.
With every moment, the magic unfolds,
A story of warmth in the bitter cold.

Celebrate life with every breath,
In twilight's glow, we dance with depth.
Cups raised high, to laughter and cheer,
The stillness sings, our hearts draw near.

As stars twinkle in the velvet sky,
We gather, we love, we wonder why.
Together we find our festive flame,
In winter's heart, the stillness knows our name.

## Wings Whispering Over Winter Slumber

In the hush of night, delicate wings,
Whisper tales of the joy that spring brings.
Over landscapes, where frost gently lays,
A lullaby hums through the festive haze.

Crystals shimmer as bright as stars,
Embracing the world with radiant scars.
With every flake, a wish takes flight,
Wings of wonder in the moonlight.

Celebrate warmth 'neath the frosty sky,
With hearts entwined, we softly sigh.
In the embrace of winter's sweet dream,
Together we bloom, like daisies in cream.

From snow-kissed rooftops to laughter below,
In every heartbeat, festive colors flow.
Wings whispering secrets, calm and deep,
In the heart of winter, our spirits leap.

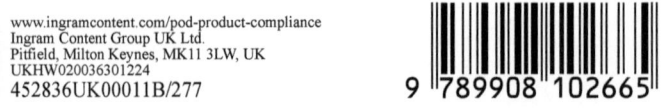